Telephone Courtesy & Customer Service

Third Edition

Lloyd Finch

A Fifty-Minute™ Series Book

CRISP. Learning

Menlo Park, California

1-800-442-7477

CrispLearning.com

Telephone Courtesy & Customer Service

Third Edition

Lloyd Finch

CREDITS:
Editor: **Debbie Woodbury**
Copy Editor: **Charlotte Bosarge**
Production Manager: **Judy Petry**
Text Design: **Amy Shayne**
Cover Design: **Amy Shayne & 5th Street Design**
Artwork: **Ralph Mapson**
Production Artist: **Kay Green**

© 1987, 2000 Crisp Publications, Inc.
Printed in the United States of America by Von Hoffmann Graphics, Inc.

CrispLearning.com

02 03   10 9 8 7 6 5 4 3

Library of Congress Catalog Card Number 99-69990
Finch, Lloyd
Telephone Courtesy & Customer Service
Third Edition
ISBN 1-56052-577-0

Learning Objectives For:

TELEPHONE COURTESY & CUSTOMER SERVICE

The objectives for *Telephone Courtesy & Customer Service, Third Edition,* are listed below. They have been developed to guide you, the reader, to the core issues covered in this book.

THE OBJECTIVES OF THIS BOOK ARE:

❏ 1) To describe the basics of providing high-quality customer service

❏ 2) To explain proper telephone skills

❏ 3) To explore the importance of understanding customer needs

❏ 4) To explain the essential role customer service plays in creating a favorable impression of the company

ASSESSING YOUR PROGRESS

In addition to the learning objectives, Crisp Learning has developed an assessment that covers the fundamental information in this book. A 25–item, multiple-choice true-false questionnaire allows the reader to evaluate his or her comprehension of the subject matter. To learn how to obtain a copy of this assessment please call **1-800-442-7477** and ask to speak with a customer service representative.

Assessments should not be used in any employee selection process.

Contents

Part 3: Understanding Customer Needs

Part 4: Managing the Customer's Perception

Preface

Welcome to *Telephone Courtesy & Customer Service*. This book is about the important telephone skills that help produce excellent customer service. You have been given this book because you are an important provider of customer service for your organization. The skills and ideas presented in this book will help you deliver an even stronger job performance.

This book has been written so that you can complete it in a relatively short time. The important thing is to read the material carefully, understand it, and apply it to your job.

There are four sections in this book. Part 1 defines a quality customer service provider, and discusses service responsibility. Part 2 discusses telephone skills and their importance to providing quality service. Part 3 explains customer "wants and needs" and describes the importance of a positive attitude. Part 4 teaches the reader how to manage customer perceptions.

Keep this book near your work location for reference. By using it regularly you will learn correct telephone skills and develop the personal skills required to provide the best possible customer service.

Applying the telephone customer service skills in this book will help you become a professional provider of quality customer service. This should be your objective.

Get out your pencil, relax, and enjoy this book.

Lloyd Finch

P A R T 1

Quality Customer Service

2

You Play a Key Role

An employee who provides quality customer service, whether for external or internal customers, must do three things:

1. Accept responsibility for providing timely customer service in a courteous manner.

2. Understand that the success of the organization depends on the level of service provided.

3. Learn and apply customer service skills in a positive manner.

Often employees are so busy there is little time to think about their jobs or how they relate to the overall success of the company. Sometimes, those who spend much of their day on the telephone talking with customers don't consider their jobs to be very important. The fact is that anyone regularly involved with customers has one of the most important jobs in that organization. Following are some points to consider:

➤ Customers will take their business elsewhere when they aren't satisfied. Customers will not continue to do business with you unless they are treated in a courteous and professional manner.

➤ Anyone working directly with customers occupies a position of trust.

➤ Organizations known for providing outstanding service acquired that reputation through the consistent efforts of people like you.

Customer Service Is Everyone's Responsibility

When we think about customer service, it is common to think that certain individuals or work groups are responsible for providing service. However, in most organizations customer service departments represent only a portion of the overall service responsibility. Everyone from CEO to shipping clerk provides customer service and contributes to an organization's reputation for service and courtesy.

If all employees learned to provide the service concepts in this book, their individual organization's reputations for quality service would improve.

In the next few pages, you will learn about successful telephone skills that will help you become even more professional when speaking on the telephone with external and internal customers.

This book offers skills, ideas, and suggestions for improving the service you provide. Put them into practice.

QUESTION: Dave is a lobby receptionist for Acme Systems. His responsibilities include registering and providing security badges for all non-employees who enter the building. Is Dave responsible for customer service?

ANSWER: You bet!

The Importance of the Telephone Within Your Organization

In your job you may use email, fax, voicemail, and the telephone. Each of these tools can help you satisfy your customers. (We will talk about managing technology later in this book.)

Although there are salespeople and others who meet with customers, most service in the typical organization is provided over the telephone.

What is your organization like?

Think for a moment about all the customer contact that occurs where you work.

1.   What percentage of all customer service is managed on the telephone?

2.   What percentage do you think is handled in face-to-face meetings?

3.   Who has more responsibility for satisfying customers?

    ❏   those who meet face-to-face with customers

    ❏   managers and supervisors

    ❏   those who speak with customers on the telephone

EXERCISE: WHO IS RESPONSIBLE FOR QUALITY CUSTOMER SERVICE?

Rate the overall contribution to customer service by the various work groups listed below. Write in a 1 for the largest contributor, a 2 for the second-largest contributor, and so forth. If your organization doesn't have a particular work group, don't rate it. But if you have the work group, it must be rated.

___ **the shipping and receiving group**

___ **the sales group**

___ **the customer service group**

___ **technical support**

___ **service technicians**

___ **telephone receptionists**

___ **managers and supervisors**

___ **order processing**

___ **lobby attendants**

___ **accounting**

___ **others**

Although one or two groups probably stand out, it is important to realize that nearly everyone has some responsibility for satisfying customers. Also, look at your selections and note how much of your service is provided over the telephone. This is why telephone skills are so important.

DIAGRAM OF A QUALITY-CONSCIOUS COMPANY

The diagram below illustrates how a customer is viewed by the best customer service companies.

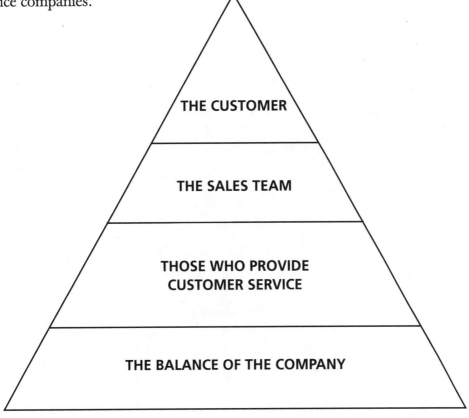

Please notice that customers are at the top of the pyramid and are supported by sales, customer service, and the balance of the organization. Keep this diagram in mind as you learn about telephone skills that can help provide quality customer service.

Proper Telephone Skills

Skill 1: Handling the Telephone

Features of the telephone need to be understood. These features are designed to help you handle calls smoothly. At first glance they may seem complicated but normally are easy to use. To understand the capabilities of your telephone better, read about the available features or ask a more experienced person to explain them to you. Then practice until they become automatic.

Joan needed to transfer a caller to a co-worker. She wasn't sure how to do it. After quickly reading the instructions Joan made the transfer, but the caller was accidentally disconnected. If Joan had spent a few minutes practicing the call transfer feature, the disconnect would have not occurred.

➤ The time to learn about your telephone is ahead of time. Do not practice on the caller. Be familiar with all of the features.

➤ Hold the transmitter portion of the telephone directly in front of your mouth. If the transmitter is held away from your mouth, you risk not being understood.

   Keep in mind that speaking on the telephone requires better articulation than is necessary in face-to-face conversations.

➤ Place the telephone on your desk so the receiver will be picked up without banging into anything. No one likes unnecessary noise.

➤ Avoid side conversations while talking on the telephone. Your party deserves your full attention. Do not attempt to carry on two conversations at the same time.

➤ Make sure you place the caller on hold before discussing his or her situation with a co-worker.

   Wouldn't it be embarrassing if you told a co-worker that a caller didn't sound too smart, only to discover that he or she was listening?

➤ Never eat or drink while talking. If your mouth is full when the telephone rings, wait a few seconds before answering.

Skill 1 (CONTINUED)

➤ Answer in as few rings as possible. A maximum of three rings is a good standard.

   Some organizations have a "three-ring policy." Check to see if yours does.

➤ Before you place a caller on hold to answer another line, ask for permission and *wait for an answer.*

   Example: *"Would you mind holding for a moment? Wait for the customer to say, "Sure, go ahead." Too often customers hears, "Please hold" and the person is gone.*

➤ If you have several callers on hold, remember the priority of each call. If necessary, make notes of who has been holding on which line and for how long.

   Nothing is more irritating than to answer the question, "Who are you holding for?" several times. When you forget who the caller was holding for, simply apologize. "I'm sorry, who were you holding for?"

Skill 2: Mastering Voice Inflection

Are you interested in the way you sound? Try this inflection exercise by speaking into a tape recorder. Read the following sentence in your normal voice:

"Michael didn't show up for work this morning."

➤ Now restate the same sentence with surprise in your voice.

➤ Try it again, but this time make it a casual statement.

➤ Next, make it sound like a secret.

➤ Finally, turn it into a question.

If done properly, as your inflection changes, the sentence will convey a completely different meaning to the listener.

14

Skill 3: Using Your Best Voice

Each of us has a unique voice. To a great extent, out voices reflect who we are. Learning how to use your voice to the best ability is possible for anyone.

The voice you project is determined by four factors, all of which can be controlled.

ENERGY — The energy in your voice reflects your attitude and enthusiasm.

RATE OF SPEECH — A normal rate is 125 words a minute. Speaking faster can create problems.

PITCH — This can be a monotone, a low, or a high pitch. Ideally you should vary your tone and inflection.

QUALITY — The above three factors make up your voice quality.

There are several things you can do to produce a more desirable speaking voice. Some include:

1. **You can warm up your voice by humming quietly. This will help deepen the sound of your voice.**

2. **Practicing your pitch and control by calling a telephone recording device and delivering several messages. Then listen to the playback and critique yourself or ask a friend to help.**

3. **Role-play with a friend and tape-record the conversation. Review it for tone, rate of delivery, and so on.**

4. **Take a speech class in a local college or through adult education.**

5. *Put a smile into your voice.* **It is easy to do. Simply remember to smile as you answer a call. Believe it or not, your voice will sound friendlier.**

EXERCISE: VOICE SELF-ASSESSMENT

Your voice reflects your personality. If it needs improvement, you can do it, but you must be willing to try. Practicing voice skills is no different than practicing a sport. If you stay at it, you are bound to improve.

Rate your voice using the following self-evaluation. Check those characteristics that apply to you and then ask a friend to help evaluate your responses.

DESIRABLE TRAITS	UNDESIRABLE TRAITS
My voice...	**My voice...**
❏ is pleasant-sounding	❏ is nasal
❏ has pitch variations	❏ sounds throaty
❏ has a normal rate	❏ is raspy
❏ varies in volume	❏ sometimes squeaks
❏ has distinct articulation	❏ is a boring monotone
❏ sounds like I am smiling	❏ is too soft
❏ has ample force	❏ is too loud
❏ stresses proper accents	❏ has too many pauses
	❏ does not convey a smile

For any undesirable traits checked, you should begin work on correcting them. The skills suggested in this book should help, but you may also want to enroll in a speech improvement class.

Skill 4: Addressing the Caller

Rules about how to address callers can be confusing because of the many options. Therefore, the following may help.

There are seven basic ways to address a calling party.

Mr.	Miss	First Name	Ms.	Sir	Mrs.	Ma'am

The average caller may or may not be sensitive about how he or she is addressed. To be on the safe side, keep these suggestions in mind:

1. When addressing a male, you are always correct to use Mr. or Sir.

2. Addressing a woman is more confusing. The use of Mrs. or Miss is common and generally acceptable. Some women prefer Ms. and may request this form of address. If you are uncertain, simply ask the caller for her preference. (Shall I address you as Miss or Mrs.? Is it Mrs. or Miss? Is it Miss or Ms. Taylor?)

3. Often when you ask for the correct form of address the caller will suggest the use of a first name. The use of the customer's first name is then acceptable. Use of a first name may also be acceptable (but not always) when:

    ➤ You have established a good rapport over a period of time.

    ➤ You have been called by your first name.

    ➤ You know the caller and know that the person is comfortable with a first-name basis.

Skill 5: Answering the Telephone

First impressions are important. Callers begin to form their impression of an organization by:

> ➤ **The number of rings it takes to get an answer**

> ➤ **The first voice they hear**

Whether the voice is live or part of voicemail it needs to help create a favorable impression. Imagine a cheerful "Good morning, Alpha Company, Cindy Jones, how may I help you?" versus a terse, clipped "International Gourmet, please hold."

The rules for answering a telephone are simple but they need to be reviewed and practiced continually. Following are the most basic ones, which should always be employed.

1. **Use the four answering courtesies.**

2. **Be enthusiastic when you answer.**

3. **Use friendly phrases as part of your greeting.**

4. **Remember to smile as you pick up the receiver.**

Skill 5 (CONTINUED)

1 Use the four answering courtesies:

➤ Greet the caller.

➤ State your organization (or department).

➤ Introduce yourself.

➤ Offer your help.

Example: *"Good afternoon, Accounting, Mary Jones speaking. How may I help you?"*

A common objection to the use of the four answering courtesies is the time it takes. If you are a receptionist answering a high volume of calls you might reduce the message to: "Good morning, Media Company, how may I help you?"

But for all other situations, the four courtesies should be used. After all, it only takes about three seconds. Try it; time yourself. Remember, the customer's perception of you and your organization begins with how you answer the telephone.

2 Be enthusiastic when you answer. Help make the calling party feel truly welcome.

A tired voice lacking in enthusiasm is unappealing.

3 Use friendly phrases as part of your greeting.

Example: *"Thanks for calling."*

"How may I help you?"

"How are you today?"

4 Remember to smile as you pick up the receiver.

TIP: *Tape the word "smile" on your telephone receiver.*

Skill 6: Practicing Effective Listening

The first lesson in listening is to be aware that there are only three types of expressions you hear from callers.

Callers will:

1. Make statements

2. Offer objections, *or*

3. Ask questions

When you fail to listen closely:

1. You will hear what you want to hear.

2. You will hear what you expect to hear.

3. You will not recognize the difference between a statement, objection, or question.

If you do not listen closely, you may not be able to understand what the call is about. For example:

Customer statement: *"Your prices are a little higher than I thought they would be."*

Close your eyes and imagine a customer making this remark. How would you interpret it? Check (✔) one.

❏ The customer has an objection.

❏ The customer made a statement.

❏ The customer has asked a question.

Answer: *The customer was making a statement.*

Skill 6 (CONTINUED)

Let's see how Megan, a professional service representative, would respond to the statement on the previous page.

> **Customer:** *"Your prices are a little higher than I thought they would be."*

> **Megan:** *"Our prices are comparable to the industry and our products have the best reputation. May I proceed with the billing information?*

Megan acknowledged the statement and then moved the conversation to the next step. If Megan had not been listening closely, she might have misinterpreted the statement as an objection or a question. For example, suppose Megan had interpreted the customer's statement as an objection. Her response might have gone like this.

> **Customer:** *"Your prices are a little higher than I thought they would be."*

> **Megan:** *"Our prices are very competitive. In fact, we lowered some prices this year."*

> **Customer:** *"They seem high to me."*

> **Megan:** *"If you compared our prices with our competitors, you would find that on the average we are very competitive."*

> **Customer:** *"Who are your major competitors?"*

In this example, Megan allowed the conversation to become a discussion regarding prices and competitors. Megan lost control simply because she handled a statement as if it were an objection.

Exercise: Are You a Good Listener?

Answer the following by checking (✔) either yes or no.

1. I frequently have to ask callers to repeat information.
   ❏ yes ❏ no

2. Are the messages or notes you take often incorrect?
   ❏ yes ❏ no

3. Do you often forget a caller's name?
   ❏ yes ❏ no

4. I sometimes forget who I placed on hold.
   ❏ yes ❏ no

5. Do you sometimes find yourself responding to the wrong question?
   ❏ yes ❏ no

6. I am easily distracted when talking on the telephone.
   ❏ yes ❏ no

7. After I hang up, I sometimes forget some of what was said.
   ❏ yes ❏ no

8. When the call is long I often have trouble concentrating.
   ❏ yes ❏ no

9. I often don't hear some of the details of the call.
   ❏ yes ❏ no

10. While listening, I mostly think about what I am going to say when it is my turn to talk.
    ❏ yes ❏ no

A perfect score is 10 "no" answers. Eight or more "no" answers is good. If you circled seven or fewer "no" answers, your listening needs some work.

HOW TO IMPROVE YOUR LISTENING

1. Listen for statements, objections, and questions.

2. Take notes as you listen, especially during longer conversations.

3. When in doubt as to what was said, ask a question.

4. Focus only on the purpose of the original conversation and avoid side conversations.

5. During longer conversations, use confirming statements to stay involved.

    Examples: *"I understand."*

    "I agree."

    "I see."

6. During longer conversations, ask questions. This will help you stay involved and help direct the conversation as well.

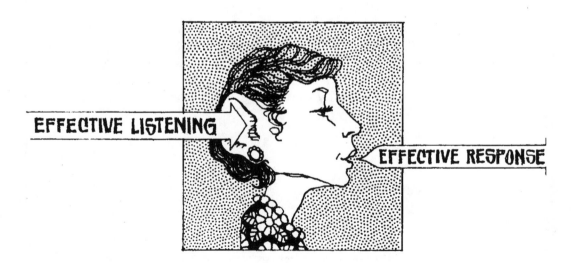

Skill 7: Managing Objections

An objection occurs when the caller is opposed to the proposed plan of action. When you hear an objection, it is important to address it immediately. If the caller offers an objection and you ignore it, you may have lost a customer.

Customer: (objection) *"Your prices seem high and I think I should shop around and compare prices before I place my order."*

Doug: *"I am sure that you will be satisfied with our product. Will a Friday delivery date be okay?"*

In this example, Doug was not listening. He did not hear the customer's objection and as a result tried to move the sale along. Doug deserves credit for trying to get the order but there is not much point when the customer's objection goes unanswered.

Most of us do not like objections. We sometimes think that if objections are ignored they will go away. They will not. Objections require an immediate reply.

Customer: (objection) *"I think I should compare prices before placing an order."*

Megan: *"That's fine. Our customers tell us we are very price competitive. We recently lowered prices on the model you are considering and it continues to carry the best warranty in the industry. If you place your order now, we could deliver it early next week."*

Skill 7 (CONTINUED)

If you ignore objections or questions, callers will usually:

- Stop you and repeat the objection or the question.

- Not say anything to you but still be dissatisfied because you ignored their concern.

When listening, always pay attention to voice inflection. It communicates a great deal. Suppose the customer says, "Your delivery dates are unbelievable." If the customer made this statement in an assertive voice, you would interpret it as an objection. If delivered in a cheerful voice, the customer has probably paid a compliment. Callers will let you know when they object to something, and their objections will usually be direct and to the point. Your job is to listen closely.

SUMMARY
MANAGING OBJECTIONS

1. Listen to what the caller says.

2. Always provide an immediate response.

3. State the response in clear and positive terms.

4. Do not provide unnecessary information and conversation.

On the following page is an exercise to help you learn to distinguish between statements, questions and objections. This activity should help you to become a more sensitive listener.

STATEMENT, QUESTION, OR OBJECTION?

In the following exercise, read each expression as if it has just been delivered to you on the telephone. Then indicate if you think it is:

S = STATEMENT   Q = QUESTION   O = OBJECTION

For expressions that are both questions and objections, write both letters in order of your ranking.

Assume all responses have been made in a normal tone of voice (you will notice that all punctuation has purposely been left out).

____ 1. I think your service is quite good

____ 2. Your delivery intervals are certainly long enough

____ 3. Why does the bill show $107.00

____ 4. Your prices are just too high for me

____ 5. You don't understand I need someone out here today

____ 6. When will it be in stock

____ 7. What are you doing about the backlog

____ 8. I can't wait I need to talk with her today

____ 9. Why is he never around when I need him

____ 10. I am not going to pay that bill

ANSWERS:

1. Statement	4. Question	8. Objection
2. Objection, Statement	5. Objection	9. Objection, Question
3. Statement	6. Question	10. Objection
	7. Question	

Skill 8: Learning the Art of Negotiation

Often you will have to negotiate with a customer. Negotiating involves recognizing the needs of the caller, comparing them against your organization's ability to deliver what is required, then reaching a solution that will satisfy both parties. Negotiation is required when a request is made for service you cannot or do not offer.

Negotiation _____

Reaching a compromise that is acceptable to both your organization and the caller.

_____

Negotiation begins with *Action Issues*. These are concerns or requests that need to be met in order to satisfy the caller.

Successful negotiation* does not mean offering a service your company cannot provide. Instead it means the ability to reach a compromise that is acceptable to both your organization and the caller.

To illustrate some negotiation skills, let's listen in on a conversation between Kwong and a customer.

> **Customer:** *"This is Bob Martin calling. I must speak with Mrs. Sims right now."*
>
> **Kwong:** *"I'm sorry, sir, but she is on another call. May I help you or take your telephone number and have her call you back?"*
>
> **Customer:** *"No, I can't wait. Interrupt her and let her know that I must speak to her."*

Kwong has an assertive customer who is demanding to talk with Mrs. Sims.

Kwong knows that Mrs. Sims is already on an important call and does not want to be interrupted.

In this situation there is a conflict between what the customer wants and what Kwong can provide. Usually in this type of situation there is room for negotiation.

If you were confronted with this situation, what would you do to provide a compromise the customer would accept?

_____

* For more information on negotiation, read <u>Successful Negotiation</u> by Robert B. Maddux, Crisp Publications, 1995.

Here are some tips:

1 **Ask questions to determine the problem.**

2 **When you select a course of action, be direct and specific in your statements.**

3 **Remain positive and service-oriented.**

If you were Kwong, how would you respond to the following customer?

Customer: *"No, I can't wait. Interrupt and let her know that I must speak to her."*

Response: _____

_____

_____

_____

_____

_____

Read the following page to see how Kwong negotiated with the customer.

KWONG NEGOTIATES

Customer: *"No, I can't wait. Interrupt and let her know that I must speak with her."*

Kwong: *"Sir, I'm sure Mrs. Sims would like to talk to you, but since she is not available, please explain what you need and I'll either personally take care of it or find someone to help you. Will that be okay?"*

Customer: *"Well, maybe you can help. Our system has been down for about two hours."*

Kwong: *"Did you call our service department?"*

Customer: *"Yes, I did."*

Kwong: *"What did they say?"*

Customer: *"One of your technicians was to have been here by ten o'clock. He has not shown up. I can't reach your service department because the lines are constantly busy."*

Kwong: *"I'll call the service department and find out what they are doing about your problem. Will you hold for a moment?"*

Customer: *"Okay."*

Kwong calls the service department and learns the technician was delayed at another location and will not be at Mr. Martin's for another hour.

Kwong: *"Mr. Martin, I talked with the supervisor in the customer service department and she said your technician has been delayed but will be there within the hour. I will check back regularly to make certain the technician will go directly to your company to meet his new deadline. I will also inform Mrs. Sims that you called. Will that be all right?"*

Customer: *"I guess so."*

Kwong: *"Thanks for your patience, Mr. Martin."*

Customer: *"Okay, thanks for your help."*

Reviewing Kwong's Course of Action

Obviously, the customer is not completely satisfied. He would like the technician to be at his business immediately, but since this is not possible, an alternate plan was arranged and he has agreed to it.

Let's review Kwong's course of action.

1. He raised his voice slightly to become more assertive.

2. By asking questions, he learned what the customer needed.

3. He proposed a course of action.

4. He was direct and specific in his statements.

In most service situations, an acceptable compromise can be reached through negotiation. Since you control the service, you are in a position to suggest a compromise or make another arrangement.

Kwong had two *action issues* to cope with:

1. The customer demanded to speak with Mrs. Sims.

2. The customer wanted a technician immediately.

Kwong knew Mrs. Sims was not available. He also knew she would not be able to get the technician to the customer's location immediately. Despite this, he took positive action, presented a plan, and asked that the customer accept it.

When you control service you must be careful with your statements to avoid coming on too strong. Even though you cannot always provide what the customer wants, it is important to deliver the response in a courteous manner.

Skill 9: Making the Service Follow-up Call

Following up on the service you provide is a professional way to conduct business. In the situation you just read, Kwong or Mrs. Sims should follow up with Mr. Martin to see if he is satisfied. Many customer service providers do not regularly follow up. They claim they do not have time. Even when it is impossible to follow up with every customer, there are certain situations in which it should be done. A few examples include:

Situations for a Follow-up Call

Nothing Went Right

Sometimes you have a situation in which, despite everyone's best effort, nothing goes right. Once the problems have been corrected, the customer should be called to determine whether everything is satisfactory. The customer will usually appreciate this courtesy.

The Irate Customer

When you hang up from a conversation with an irate customer, the last thing you want to do is speak with that customer again. Whether the cause of the complaint was legitimate or questionable, a follow-up call is a good idea. By calling to ask if the action you initiated was satisfactory, the customer will be pleasantly surprised to hear from you and perhaps will become a good customer.

A New Customer

When you establish a new account or provide service to a new customer, it's a good time to extend an extra courtesy. Make a follow-up call to learn if everything is satisfactory. It will enhance the customer's perception of your company and make repeat business more likely.

The Regular Customer

Those who do business with you deserve occasional follow-up calls. It is easy to take regular customers for granted. An occasional friendly follow-up service call tells regular customers "we care about you."

Never hesitate to make a follow-up service call. Even when the customer was irate or the service you provided did not go as planned, call. It is always better to know the level of customer satisfaction than guess at it. If a customer continues to have a problem, you need to know about it so it can be corrected. And when the customer does not have a problem, the follow-up call will be appreciated even more.

Skill 10: Asking Questions

Often you are required to ask questions to get information you need. There are two types of questions that can be used and each has a particular purpose. The types are *open questions* and *closed questions*.

OPEN QUESTIONS	can be used when you want a customer to explain or discuss something
CLOSED QUESTIONS	should be used when all you need is a "yes" or "no"

For example, if you ask a customer, "Did you receive the shipment?" The answer will be either "yes" or "no". However, if you want the customer to discuss the particulars of the shipment, you could ask instead, "What was the condition of the shipment when it arrived?" This way when the customer answers, an explanation is required.

Use both types of questions to gain better control of your telephone conversations.

At the beginning of most customer calls you need to learn what the customer wants, so you would use *open* questions. Later, you may need to employ *closed* questions to get the customer's agreement, to understand a service request, or just to manage the conversation and your time.

TIP: *It is also possible to* **shorten** *telephone calls by effectively using open and closed questions.*

Skill 10 (CONTINUED)

Open Questions

Open questions begin with the words: **How, Why, When, Who, What, and Where**

Examples: *"How often does that happen?"*

"What did you do before the problem started?"

"Who is responsible for your billing?"

"When did the package arrive?"

Closed Questions

Closed questions begin with words like: **Did, Can, Have, Do, Is, Will, and Would**

Examples: *"Did you call them?"*

"Do you have your bill?"

"Have you received our refund?"

"Will you attend our seminar?"

"May I do that for you?"

Any statement can be "closed" by following it with a question.

Examples: *"I would like to send you a brochure about our services.* ***Will that be okay?"***

"You will call me back before four o'clock today. ***Is that correct?"***

Closing for Agreement, Clarification, or to Manage Time

Other examples of closed questions you can use at the end of statements include:

> *"Do you approve?"*

> *"Will you participate?"*

> *"Is that a good time to call?"*

> *"Will that be all right?"*

Short closed questions can also be used to obtain the customer's agreement. For example:

> *"Our technician will be there on Friday. **Will that be okay?**"*

> *"We have to bill you for that service. **Is that all right?**"*

> *"I will call you 10:00 A.M. Monday morning. **Will you be available?**"*

These examples sound like you are giving the customer a choice. However, you are basically asking for a confirmation of your statement.

Suppose you were arranging an appointment for one of your sales representatives. The only open date you had to offer was Tuesday at nine o'clock. You could say:

> *"I'm sorry, Miss Johnson, but the only date Mr. Stevens has open is Tuesday at nine o'clock. **I hope that will be okay.**"*

This statement is poorly phrased. It could be stated more positively if you said:

> *"Miss Johnson, I have arranged for our sales representative Mr. Stevens to visit you on Tuesday at nine o'clock. **Will that be all right?**"*

The customer might still request a different date; however, your statement sounds like you have taken positive action.

Skill 10 (CONTINUED)

When to Use Open or Closed Questions

When gathering information, keep the following in mind. It will help you determine when to use *open* or *closed* questions.

IF YOU NEED TO...	USE
Determine problems, understand requests, or establish needs	*open questions*
Ask callers to explain requests or problems	*open questions*
Ask for more information to determine a course of action	*both open and closed questions*
Get agreement	*closed questions*

KEY WORDS	
OPEN	**CLOSED**
HOW	DID
WHY	CAN
WHEN	HAVE
WHO	DO
WHAT	WILL/WOULD
WHERE	IS

TIP: *Copy this page and keep it near your phone to remind you when to use open or closed questions.*

EXERCISE: OPEN AND CLOSED QUESTIONS

Take a few minutes to complete the following exercise on open and closed questions. Identify the questions below as either *closed* or *open* by writing the appropriate letter in the space provided. Answers are on the next page.

C = CLOSED   O = OPEN

_____ 1. What did you do with the disk?

_____ 2. Where did the customer's paperwork go?

_____ 3. Have you paid the bill?

_____ 4. We need the payment by Friday. Will that be okay?

_____ 5. How much work is required?

_____ 6. Can it be fixed?

_____ 7. Is the customer holding?

_____ 8. How many calls did we make today?

_____ 9. Why did our incoming calls stop at three o'clock?

_____ 10. Ms. Jones is happy with our service. Isn't she?

_____ 11. Why didn't you test it?

_____ 12. Will you call me?

_____ 13. How long have you been at your current location?

_____ 14. Do you want to have lunch?

_____ 15. Customers are always right. Aren't they?

_____ 16. Did the boss tell you to do that?

_____ 17. What is the latest inventory level?

_____ 18. They were pretty high. Weren't they?

_____ 19. Closed questions are answered with a yes or no. Isn't that true?

_____ 20. Why do open questions begin with words like how, why, when, where, and what?

OPEN AND CLOSED QUESTIONS: ANSWER KEY

	ANSWER	REASON
1.	O	question begins with *what*
2.	O	question begins with *where*
3.	C	question begins with *have*
4.	C	ends with a closed question
5.	O	question begins with *how*
6.	C	question begins with *can*
7.	C	questions begins with *is*
8.	O	questions begins with *how*
9.	O	question begins with *why*
10.	C	ends with a closed question
11.	O	question begins with *why*
12.	C	question begins with *will*
13.	O	question begins with *how*
14.	C	question begins with *do*
15.	C	ends with a closed question
16.	C	question begins with *did*
17.	O	question begins with *what*
18.	C	ends with a closed question
19.	C	ends with a closed question
20.	O	question begins with *why*

To improve your use of open and closed questions, practice is required. *Don't you agree?* (Closed)

Skill 11: Making the Outbound Service Call

Anytime you call a customer, there are important steps to follow. Even though you may not be calling to sell a product, the basic steps of a successful telemarketing call still apply.

Before you make your call, develop an action plan:

1. Greet the customer in a friendly way.

2. Introduce yourself and your company.

3. State the purpose of the call.

4. Deliver your message in friendly, clear, and businesslike terms, leaving room for questions.

5. State any customer benefits.

6. Ask for agreement.

CASE STUDY

THE OVERBOOKED SEMINAR

Cindy mistakenly overbooked a seminar. She needed to call Mrs. Stanger to explain why her seminar date had to be changed. Cindy developed the following telemarketing action plan.

HER OBJECTIVE:	Arrange a new seminar date for Mrs. Stanger.
THE APPROACH:	Briefly explain the need for the change and offer two alternate dates.
CUSTOMER BENEFITS:	The seminar will be less crowded on the new dates and Mrs. Stanger will receive more attention from the seminar leader.
CINDY:	"Good morning, Mrs. Stanger. This is Cindy Rogers from GAC. How are you today? The reason for my call is to discuss your seminar date. The date I booked for your group is too crowded. What I can do is offer a date that will be less crowded. This means you will be able to ask more questions and receive more attention from the seminar leader. I have the 16th or 20th available. Do you have a preference?"

In the situation above, Cindy did a good job because she turned a negative situation positive by planning ahead.

Skill 12: Delivering Bad News

Occasionally you will not be able to provide something that was promised. In these situations it is essential to telephone the customer to explain what has happened. Keeping a customer informed is courteous service. There will be times when it may be unpleasant to deliver bad news but it must be done.

There are two approaches you can use. We call one the *Direct Approach* and the other *Good News/Bad News*.

The Direct Approach

Example: *"Good morning, Mr. King. This is Jim West from Woodwinds Unlimited. Do you have a moment? The reason for my call is to let you know that I made a mistake when I added your bill yesterday. I quoted you $287.00 but the correct total is $337.00. I apologize for the error but wanted to insure the correct amount was okay with you."*

The Good News/Bad News Approach

Example: *"Good morning Mr. King. This is Jim West from Woodwinds Unlimited. How are you today? I wanted you to know that I confirmed our technician will visit you on Friday as scheduled. I also wanted you to know that I misquoted the service charge during our last conversation. I quoted a service charge of $125.00 and it's really $150.00. I apologize for the error and hope it won't cause problems."*

When you make an error (and we all do), it is important to accept responsibility for it. Be honest with your customer. No one likes unpleasant surprises such as unexpected billing amounts, people who do not show up, or shipments that differ from what was ordered.

Skill 13: Managing Different Caller Behaviors

Every caller is different. Experienced customer service providers learn to recognize these differences and adjust their responses accordingly in order to provide better service.

Let's look at five different types of caller behavior often heard on the telephone.

Caller Behavior Patterns

1. **Assertive/Demanding**

2. **Angry**

3. **Passive**

4. **Talkative**

5. **Analytical/Detail-Oriented**

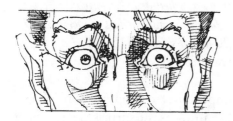

1 The Assertive/Demanding Caller

"Don't get in the swamp with the alligator."

Assertive/demanding people are pretty easy to recognize on the telephone because they are quick to show authority, demand action, and usually get the point immediately. There is seldom any mystery as to what they want because they make it clear. They spend little time with social or other non-business conversation. Their calls will generally be shorter than most because they want to get business taken care of. Does this mean they are upset or angry? No. However, it is easy to mistake their assertiveness for anger, especially if you fail to listen closely.

The difference between assertive/demanding and angry customers is the emotion involved. Angry customers are very emotional, at least at the beginning of the call. To avoid problems, it is very important not to match their emotion with your response. Instead, remain calm and stay out of the swamp, and the conversation will usually work out. Keep in mind, the assertive and the angry customer usually want to stick to business so try being less social and avoid the small talk. So unless you find they want to be social, stick to business by being direct and to the point. Here are four steps that will work for you:

Step 1. Stay objective. Do not participate in the caller's emotion.

Step 2. Listen. It is important to understand the caller's problem or concern. Sometimes it is valuable to let the caller vent his emotions, e.g., let him or her tell you how unhappy he or she is with your organization.

Step 3. Relate. Apologize in a general way or in a broad sense.

Step 4. Propose an action plan. Offer a solution that will solve the problem. Be direct in your action plan.

> **Example:** *"I'll follow up to make certain that we ship you the blue shirt and the red tie. I'll call you on Friday to make certain you received everything. Will that be okay?"*

Skill 13 (CONTINUED)

When dealing with an assertive/demanding customer on the telephone you may need to raise your assertiveness level to simply manage the conversation.

How to raise your assertiveness level:

➤ If your voice is soft, raise it slightly.

➤ Be direct and to the point in your statements.

➤ Keep the non-business conversation to a minimum.

A word of caution: keep your assertiveness level just below the caller's. Matching or exceeding the caller's assertiveness could produce an argument.

TIP: *Do not be offended by lack of rapport with this type of customer. Remember, they are interested in the business side, not the social or relationship side, of business.*

SUMMARY

RESPONDING TO AN

ASSERTIVE/DEMANDING CALLER

1. Listen so that you will understand the problem or request.

2. Match some of the caller's assertiveness.

3. Use closed questions to help control the conversation.

4. Be friendly but specific and direct in your statements.

5. Remain courteous.

2 The Angry Caller

Angry callers are a challenge even to the most experienced customer service provider. The task can be difficult but also very rewarding, especially when an angry customer calms down and actually becomes friendly.

When you have telephone contact with an irate customer, there are three important skills that will help you manage the conversation.

Skill 1: **Listen.** It is important to understand the caller's problem or concern.

Skill 2. **Relate.** Apologize in a general way or in a broad sense.

Skill 3. **Propose an action plan.** Offer a solution that will solve the problem.

Relating by Apologizing

> *"Mrs. Franz, I understand how you must feel. I'm sorry."*

> *"I'm sorry about the confusion."*

> *"Mr. Welch, I don't blame you for being upset. Let's see if we can correct the problem."*

Note that in the above example the apology is very general. You can always apologize for the situation or the confusion without admitting that you or your company were wrong. Most customers will find a general apology acceptable.

When the customer has a legitimate complaint sometimes it is best to relate by agreeing.

Relating by Agreeing

> *"Mrs. Johnson, you're right. You were promised a callback yesterday and we didn't call. Let's start again and get this problem solved."*

> *"I'm sorry, Mr. Valdez, I promised you delivery by yesterday and didn't make it. This time I promise we'll do it right."*

Skill 13 (CONTINUED)

When a customer complains, offer your concern that he or she is upset, but do not take aggressive or hostile comments personally. Remain calm and avoid getting caught up in the emotion.

Finally, once you are calm and have listened closely, it is time to offer an action plan. Make sure your action plan is one you can deliver. The action plan should be stated in clear and concise terms.

Examples of action plans:

"I'll check with accounting and call you back with an answer before four o'clock today."

"Let's do this. I'll call the technician and find out what time you can expect her and then I'll call you. Will that be okay?"

SUMMARY
TELEPHONE SKILLS FOR MANAGING
THE ANGRY CALLER

1. Avoid the caller's emotion. (Don't get in the swamp with the alligator.)

2. Listen closely so you will understand the problem.

3. Relate by apologizing in a general way.

4. Propose an action plan and then follow through.

5. Remain courteous.

3 The Passive Caller

It is usually easier to provide service for a passive customer. Satisfied customers are often passive. Experience has told them they do not need to push or complain. They know they will receive the service they need.

One mistake frequently made with passive customers is to take them for granted. Because they usually don't complain we assume they are satisfied with the service received. It is not the nature of most passive people to demand service or to express anger. If they are dissatisfied with your service they may simply quit calling.

CASE STUDY

THE QUIET CUSTOMER

Jenny's supervisor asked her why the activity had dropped off on the Hodges Company account. Jenny said she wasn't sure why Mr. Hodges had quit calling. According to Jenny, "I thought Mr. Hodges was very pleased with our service. He never complained. Even when we had computer problems and his bills were incorrect he didn't say a word about it."

Jenny could have asked: "Mr. Hodges, I know your billing was incorrect last month but we have that fixed now. Have there been any other problems?"

Sometimes the passive customer may need a little prompting:

"Mr. Hodges, according to my records your shipments have been on time. Have there been any problems?"

Passive customers are often relationship-oriented. This means they typically want a relationship with their service provider. For example, they will normally exchange some social conversation during the business call. It is important to participate in order to build a stronger relationship with this customer.

TIP: *One skill that is usually successful with passive customers is to periodically ask them about your level of service.*

Skill 13 (CONTINUED)

4 The Talkative Caller

Talkative people are often interesting and enjoyable, but on the telephone they can take up a lot of time. To avoid losing valuable time, a conversation with a talkative customer must be managed. There are three proven skills that will work for you.

Skill 1: Ask closed questions.

Skill 2: Use space control.

Skill 3: Provide minimal response.

1. Ask Closed Questions

Use closed questions as often as possible with a talkative caller. The short answers you receive will help move the conversation along. Ask open questions only when you need more explanation. (See pages 31–36 for more on closed and open questions.)

2. Use Space Control

Space control sounds exotic but it simply means providing little space between your statements for the talkative customer to interrupt. You can do this and remain courteous without rushing. Between sentences use a shorter pause than normal and then immediately make your next statements or ask a question.

3. Provide Minimal Response

Do not invite unnecessary conversation. The talkative customer may want to engage you in non-business conversation. To reduce the amount of conversation, keep your responses to a minimum and always steer the conversation back to business.

Minimal response examples:

Customer: *"How is everything going? Have they been keeping you busy?"*

Jenny: *"We have been really busy. **How may I help you?**"*

Customer: *"Hi, Jenny! This is Mike. How's everything going? Did you watch the movie on cable last night?"*

Jenny: *"Hi, Mike. No, I missed the movie but I heard it was good. **What can I do for you?**"*

5 The Analytical/Detail-Oriented Caller

The analytical caller is primarily focused on accuracy. He or she wants want the facts of the situation and is often interested in a detailed response. For example, it might be acceptable to tell an assertive customer that you will take care of the problem and call him or her back, and leave it at that. But the analytical type wants to know the who, what, why, when, and how of the situation.

Your response might sound like this:

> *I'll call our Tech Support group immediately and discuss the options you mentioned. Once they give me some feedback, I'll call you. Let's plan on a call this afternoon at four o'clock. Is that a good time for you?"*

When analytical callers have to make a decision, they want lots of information. Where as assertive customers might be very quick to say "yes" or "no" to your product or service, analytical customers will want time—time to think and analyze so that they can be accurate.

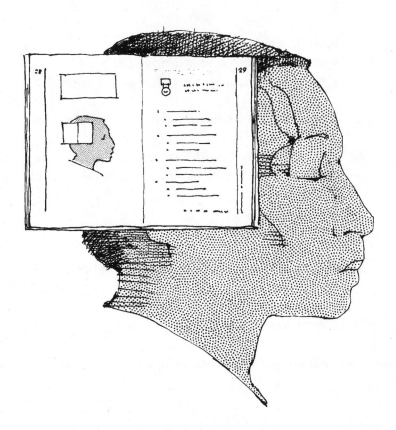

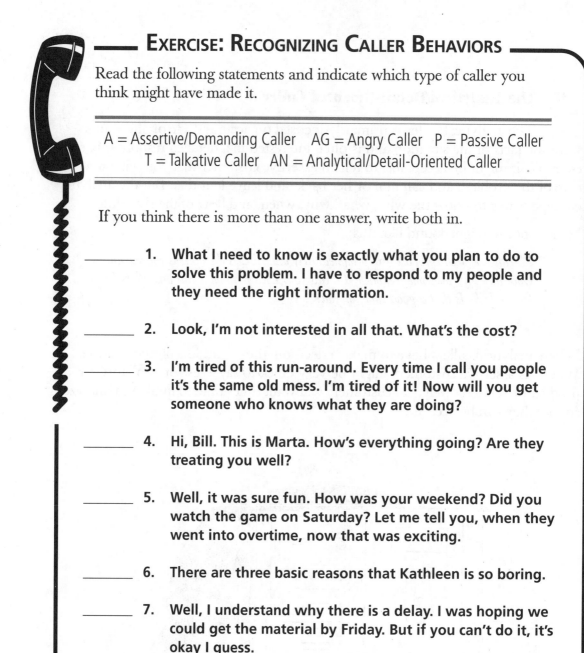

EXERCISE: RECOGNIZING CALLER BEHAVIORS

Read the following statements and indicate which type of caller you think might have made it.

A = Assertive/Demanding Caller   AG = Angry Caller   P = Passive Caller
T = Talkative Caller   AN = Analytical/Detail-Oriented Caller

If you think there is more than one answer, write both in.

_____ 1. What I need to know is exactly what you plan to do to solve this problem. I have to respond to my people and they need the right information.

_____ 2. Look, I'm not interested in all that. What's the cost?

_____ 3. I'm tired of this run-around. Every time I call you people it's the same old mess. I'm tired of it! Now will you get someone who knows what they are doing?

_____ 4. Hi, Bill. This is Marta. How's everything going? Are they treating you well?

_____ 5. Well, it was sure fun. How was your weekend? Did you watch the game on Saturday? Let me tell you, when they went into overtime, now that was exciting.

_____ 6. There are three basic reasons that Kathleen is so boring.

_____ 7. Well, I understand why there is a delay. I was hoping we could get the material by Friday. But if you can't do it, it's okay I guess.

_____ 8. Just give me the numbers, okay?

_____ 9. Listen, before we talk about that, let me tell you what happened to me.

_____ 10. The answer is no!

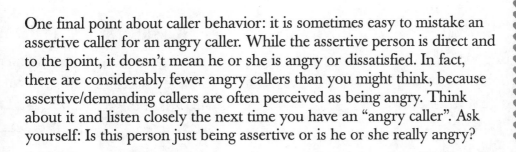

ANSWERS: RECOGNIZING CALLER BEHAVIORS

1. AN	6. AN
2. A	7. P
3. AG	8. A
4. P or T	9. T
5. T	10. A

One final point about caller behavior: it is sometimes easy to mistake an assertive caller for an angry caller. While the assertive person is direct and to the point, it doesn't mean he or she is angry or dissatisfied. In fact, there are considerably fewer angry callers than you might think, because assertive/demanding callers are often perceived as being angry. Think about it and listen closely the next time you have an "angry caller". Ask yourself: Is this person just being assertive or is he or she really angry?

50

Skill 14: Managing Telephone Messages

When you manage a volume of incoming calls or are away from your desk, telephone messages often pile up. If there are many messages, priorities need to be established and to do so requires organization on your part, especially when there is limited time in which to return these calls.

Determining in what order calls should be returned is an important decision. For example, suppose you had eight messages.

The messages were:

MEMO	**MEMO**	**MEMO**	**MEMO**
Customer John Stanley called twice. He says it's urgent. ❶	Your friend Michelle called. ❷	Customer R. Bliss called. He has some questions. ❸	Customer Joyce Smith called. Has an order to place. ❹
Mike from accounting called. Has a question. ❺	Ron called. Please confirm your report will be in by Tuesday. ❻	Mrs. Davis called. Has a question regarding the company picnic. ❼	Customer Jim Oates called. Must speak with you ASAP. ❽

One easy method of determining message priority is quickly comparing one message to another. For example: Is message #1 (John Stanley) more or less important than #2 (Michelle's call)? Next compare message #1 to message #3 and decide if it is more or less important. By continuing the process the correct decisions will be reached.

Initially this process may take a few minutes, but with a little experience it can be done quickly just by glancing at each message.

THE COMPARISON METHOD

Using the comparison method, in what order would you return the preceding calls? Write in the number of the message.

1._____   5._____

2._____   6._____

3._____   7._____

4._____   8._____

ANSWERS: 1. #1 2. #8 3. #4 4. #3 5. #5 6. #6 7. #7 8. #2

Skill 15: Managing the Customer Callback

When you are unable to handle a request at the time of the original telephone call, here are four callback steps to follow:

Step 1: **Briefly explain the need for the callback.**

Step 2: **Ask for permission to make a callback.**

Step 3: **Make a commitment to call at an agreed-upon time.**

Step 4: **Personalize your statements.**

Here is an example of how to manage a customer callback:

> *"It will take some time to get that information for you, Mr. Jones. Will it be okay if I call you back this afternoon before four o'clock?"*

If we break this statement into four callback steps, it would look like this:

Step 1: Explaining the need for the callback. *"It will take some time to get that information for you...*

Step 4: Personalize your statements. *...Mr. Jones...*

Step 2: Ask for permission to make a callback. *...will it be okay if I call you back this afternoon.*

Step 3: Make a commitment to call at an agreed-upon time. *...before four o'clock?*

Another example:

> *"Mr. Jones, it's going to take a while because I want to research the material completely for you. I won't be able to call you back until tomorrow morning at 10:00 A.M. Will that be all right?"*

Step 4:	Personalize your statements explaining the need for the callback.	*"Mr. Jones...*
Step 1:	Explaining the need for the callback.	*...it's going to take a while because I want to research the material completely for you...*
Step 3:	Make a commitment to call at an back agreed-upon time.	*...I won't be able to call you until tomorrow morning at 10:00 A.M...*
Step 2:	Ask for permission to make a callback.	*...Will that be all right?"*

Remember, customers expect a fast response. When you cannot provide one, you need to commit to an action plan, including the time you will call back. Be sure to offer a return call time that you can meet. Do not compound your problem by committing to an unrealistic deadline.

Skill 16: Avoiding Statements that Give the Wrong Impression

Everything you say to a customer or a caller leaves an impression. When you make positive statements, the customer's impression is positive. When you get careless and fail to think about what you are saying, sometimes the wrong impression may be left inadvertently.

Check (✔) those statements you have heard or used yourself.

- ❏ "I'm sorry, but Maggie is still at lunch."

- ❏ "I don't know where he is. May I take your number and have him call you?"

- ❏ "I think she is still having coffee. I'll have her call you."

- ❏ "She is in the middle of a big customer problem. Would you like to leave a message?"

- ❏ "He is at the doctor's office."

- ❏ "She went home early."

- ❏ "I'm sorry, but Gene hasn't come to work yet."

- ❏ "The service person should be there on Friday."

- ❏ "Your bill should be correct now."

- ❏ "Our service department takes forever to answer the phone."

The next page contains an evaluation of these "too common" statements.

"I'm sorry, but Maggie is still at lunch."

The key word to avoid is "still." Saying "still" implies a long lunch hour.

"I don't know where he is. May I take your number and have him call you?"

You hear this a lot. When there is a call for someone and you are not sure where the person is, that information should not be shared with the caller. A simple "He is unavailable at the moment. May I have him call you?" will do fine.

"I think she is still having coffee. I'll have her call you."

Similar to statements one and two. This information need not be shared with the customer.

"She is in the middle of a big customer problem. Would you like to leave a message?"

This statements tells your caller that you have "big customer problems." Why share this type of information? Simply say, "I'm sorry, she is unavailable," and offer to take a message or to help the caller.

"He is at the doctor's office."

Do not share personal information about a co-worker with the customer. Instead, say, "He will be out of the office until three o'clock. May I help you?"

"She went home early."

Customers get furious at this one. They need help and discover the person who can help them went home early. Treat this situation as personal information and do not share it.

Skill 16 (CONTINUED)

"I'm sorry, but Gene hasn't come to work yet."

The word "yet" implies being late. Just say: "I am sorry but Mr. Smith is not available. May I help you?"

"The service person should be there on Friday."

Keep statements positive. Avoid creating doubts about your service. Change "should be there" to "will be there."

"Your bill should be correct now."

Words like "should," as compared to "will," make your statement negative. Use positive words.

"Our service department takes forever to answer the phone."

If you have internal problems, it is not a good idea to share the situation with your caller. Do not broadcast problems.

Keep in mind, when there are problems on your side, it is very unprofessional to involve the customer or to blame other people you work with for the mistake. When explaining a problem or a mistake to a customer, *keep the details of what went wrong to a minimum.* In other words, do not get the customer involved in your problems.

There are other negative telephone statements that are frequently used. You can probably list several. The point is, everything you say on the telephone influences a caller's perception of you *and* your organization.

EXERCISE: CUSTOMER PERCEPTIONS

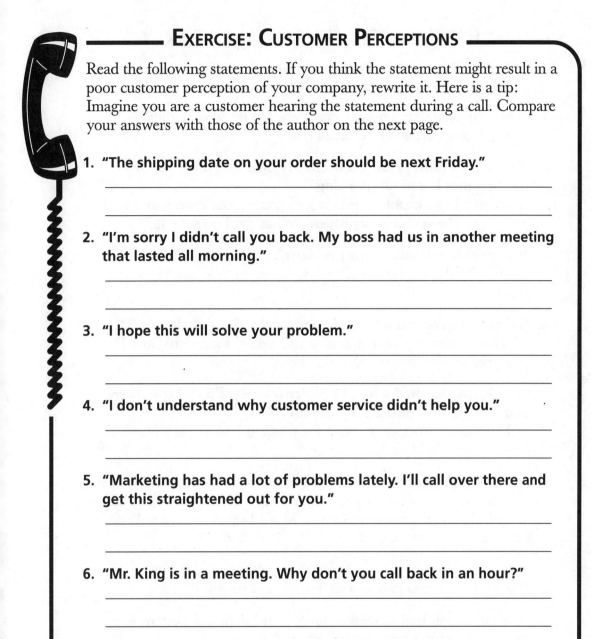

Read the following statements. If you think the statement might result in a poor customer perception of your company, rewrite it. Here is a tip: Imagine you are a customer hearing the statement during a call. Compare your answers with those of the author on the next page.

1. "The shipping date on your order should be next Friday."

2. "I'm sorry I didn't call you back. My boss had us in another meeting that lasted all morning."

3. "I hope this will solve your problem."

4. "I don't understand why customer service didn't help you."

5. "Marketing has had a lot of problems lately. I'll call over there and get this straightened out for you."

6. "Mr. King is in a meeting. Why don't you call back in an hour?"

7. "I'm sorry it took so long. Now what do you want?"

8. "I'm sorry you had to wait so long. Our telephone system is a mess and I didn't know you were on hold."

CUSTOMER PERCEPTIONS: ANSWER KEY

Your phrasing does not have to be identical with the following suggestions. If your statement is positive, it is probably correct.

1. **"The shipping date on your order should be next Friday."**
   "Your shipping date will be next Friday."

2. **"I'm sorry I didn't call you back. My boss had us in another meeting that lasted all morning."**
   "I'm sorry I was unable to get back to you sooner. How may I help you?" or "Thanks for being patient. What can I do for you?"

3. **"I hope this will solve your problem."**
   "This will solve the problem," or "Allow me to take care of the problem."

4. **"I don't understand why customer service didn't help you."** *
   "I'm sorry there has been a misunderstanding. Please hold and I'll call customer service for you. Will that be all right?"

5. **"Marketing has had a lot of problems lately. I'll call over there and get this straightened out for you."** *
   "I'll be pleased to call marketing for you and resolve your problem. Do you mind holding for a minute?"

6. **"Mr. King is in a meeting. Why don't you call back in an hour?"**
   "Mr. King is unavailable right now. May I help you?" or "Mr. King is away from his office at the moment. May I help you or would you prefer to leave a message?"

7. **"I'm sorry it took so long. Now what do you want?"**
   "I'm sorry that you had to wait. How may I help you?"

8. **"I'm sorry you had to wait so long. Our telephone system is a mess and I didn't know you were on hold."**
   "I'm sorry that you had to wait. How may I help you?" or "I apologize for the delay. "

If you find yourself using negative words, phrases, or sentences, you need to take corrective action. One simple idea is to write "POSITIVE WORDS ONLY" and tape it to your telephone. Every time you use the telephone it will serve as a reminder to communicate a positive response.

Note: There are a variety of positive statements that can be made for statements 4 and 5. The correct rephrasing should include a positive action plan for the customer.

Skill 17: Managing Technology

During a typical workday, you may use voicemail, fax, email, or even participate in a conference call. Each of these services is easy to use, but to be successful a few commonsense guidelines need to be followed.

Voicemail

Some tips for handling voicemail:

TIP 1.   Upon returning to your desk, check for messages. Return calls promptly.

TIP 2.   When leaving a message be sure that it is clear, and concise, and contains enough details to be understood. One idea behind a voicemail system is the privacy it affords, and therefore more detailed and longer messages can be left. In this way you can often avoid numerous callbacks.

TIP 3.   When you are gone for longer periods, forward your calls to someone who can help the caller, or leave instructions within your greeting stating how the caller can get help.

TIP 4.   Understand the features of your voice message system. Booklets are usually available explaining what is available, or your system administrator can answer more detailed questions.

Robert did not understand the voicemail system very well. He thought he left a personal message for a friend within his work group. By mistake he selected a broadcast code instead of the friend's mailbox number. Now everyone in his work group has heard his "personal" message.

Skill 17 (CONTINUED)

Voicemail Rights for Customers

Do you think customers are entitled to certain rights when they try to reach you? You bet they are. Here is a list of reasonable expectations when customers try to call you:

➤ When you are not available I will get a choice of leaving a message or transferring to someone who can help me now.

➤ Your personal message will tell me when you will return so that I will know approximately when I can expect a callback.

➤ When you leave me a message you will include a good time for me to call back. I'll do the same for you.

➤ Most of the time you will personally answer your telephone.

What about your customers? Do they have additional expectations? If so, what are they?

You can write your answers here:

_____

_____

_____

Suggestion: Discuss this topic within your work group.

Fax

Fax machines can be found almost everywhere now. Even though sending a fax is quick and easy, there are still some things to consider.

Brent is very careful how he speaks with customers, but he recently got a little careless with a fax. One of his important customers told him she had to change an order because of possible layoffs. Brent faxed a copy of the reduced order and wrote a note to go with it that said, "Here is your copy. Sorry to hear about the layoffs."

Brent demonstrated some poor judgment to say the least. Keep in mind that faxes are seldom private. Where is your fax machine located? Is it placed where nearly anyone could look at incoming messages? This is often the case. As a general rule always assume the customer's fax is in a large office and accessible to everyone.

TIP: *Treat fax communication just as you would a business letter. Make certain that it is professional and well written.*

Skill 17 (CONTINUED)

Email

Email is meant to be a faster and cheaper form of business communication, but far too often email is used for personal mail, jokes, and assorted trivia. It would be easy to simply overlook an important message because of all the "stuff" that clutters up email.* Here are three simple guidelines to follow when using email:

➤ Do not assume the message is private.

➤ Make your messages businesslike, clear, and concise.

➤ Do not use your business email for personal communication.

Conference Calling

Conference calling can be an easy way to communicate. There are just a few rules to follow:

➤ When the customer is participating in the conference call, make certain others on the call know it.

➤ Keep in mind, since separate speakerphones are often in use, you may not know who is listening.

➤ Because of the number of people involved during most conference calls, be even more discreet and professional.

---

* *For more on proper email procedure, read <u>The 3 R's of Email: Risks, Rights, and Responsibilities</u> by Hartman and Nantz, Crisp Publications, Inc., 1996.*

Skill 18: Closing the Conversation

When you finish your telephone conversation there are some appropriate and courteous statements that should always be made. You should:

➤ Thank the customer for calling.

➤ Let the customer know you appreciate his or her business.

➤ Provide assurance that any promises will be fulfilled.

➤ Leave the customer with a positive feeling.

Courteous Closing Statements

"Thank you for calling. We appreciate your business."

"Thanks for your order."

"Feel free to call us about anything."

"I'm glad we were able to help."

"Goodbye, and thanks for calling."

"I enjoyed talking with you."

"If you have any additional questions, please call me."

TIP: *Always let the customer hang up first. This is simple courtesy, plus it gives the caller a final chance to add something.*

Understanding Customer Needs

Take Time to Understand

Now that you have learned some important telephone skills, let's concentrate on the customer. Every customer has needs and expectations that must be met. To understand these needs, carefully complete the exercises and activities in this section.

On the following page is a conversation between Shawn, a call center trainee and his supervisor, Elaine. Make note of how you would answer if your supervisor asked the same questions Elaine is asking Shawn.

CASE STUDY

SHAWN'S CUSTOMERS

As a trainee in the call center, Shawn's job is to answer customer telephone calls, provide price quotes, and take orders. The job is hectic because of the number of calls received each day.

After a few weeks on the job, Shawn's supervisor, Elaine, met with him to discuss his job performance. Elaine began the discussion with a question.

Elaine: *"Shawn, how do you think you are doing?"*

Shawn: *"Well, pretty good I think. There is still a lot to learn but I feel I am making progress."*

Elaine: *"I agree. Your progress has been good. Let me ask you a question. How would you describe the responsibilities of your job?"*

Shawn: *"My responsibilities include handling as many customer calls as possible, making sure my orders are accurate, and knowing our products and services well."*

Elaine: *"Those are all important responsibilities and you are doing a good job in those areas."*

Shawn: *"Thanks."*

Elaine: *"How do you think you are at providing good customer service?"*

Shawn: *" I must be okay since I don't know of any customer complaints."*

Elaine: *"I don't know of any complaints either, but what type of service do you think our customers want?"*

Shawn: *"Well, I haven't thought much about it. I guess they want accurate orders and fast delivery. From what many tell me, they are not too happy with our delivery dates."*

Shawn has the potential to be a very good customer service provider. Right now, however, Shawn is like a lot of people in similar jobs. He is so busy handling customer calls that he has not had time to think about customer service.

When his supervisor asked him, "What type of service do you think our customers want?" Shawn did not have a clear understanding of his customer's service needs.

What Your Customer Wants

To understand better what your customer wants, listen to three customers explain their needs.

Suppose you asked three of your customers, "What are your service needs?" Chances are you would hear statements similar to those that follow. As you read each response, *listen* closely to what the customer has to say. Then in the space provided, write what you think the customer wants.

Customer One

"I want to be able to depend on your service. When I call and have a question or need something, I expect to be helped. I don't want to be transferred from one person to another and I don't want to just be dropped into voicemail. I'd like to talk with a real person some of the time. I also expect correct information. Whether it's a simple shipping date or something more complex, I need the right information because I am dependent on what you tell me. If I receive incorrect information, it may cause me a lot of unnecessary work. When you don't do what you promise it causes problems for me and other people in my organization. For example, if you promise a delivery date, I want to depend on that information."

Customer One Wants:

1. _____

2. _____

3. _____

4. _____

Above all else, this customer wants you to be:

Friendly? Honest? Social? Accurate? Funny?

ANSWER: Accurate

Customer Two

"When we decide to buy from a company, we consider everything: the product, the service, and the price. Most companies have an 800 number. All promise wonderful service but sometimes I feel the only service is the 800 number. I want to speak with people who know what they are doing and can help me. We like consistency. We want to receive courteous, fast service from everyone with whom we speak. I hate callbacks. I know it is not possible for someone to help me immediately every time I call, but the majority of the time we should be able to get the information we need."

Customer Two Wants:

1. _____

2. _____

3. _____

4. _____

Customer Two also mentioned three considerations when deciding to buy from a company. What are they?

1. _____

2. _____

3. _____

What Your Customer Wants (CONTINUED)

Customer Three

"My biggest complaint is people who don't listen. Sometimes it seems they are just going through the motions. If I call and explain what I want, or what I think I want, they simply seem to record the information, quote a price, and say goodbye. I'm sure there are times when suggestions could be offered to me about different alternatives. Customer service representatives should know their products and services better than I do. Another thing: I don't enjoy being put on hold. I often hear, "Please hold for a second while I check that." Then, after what seems like an eternity, I hear a live voice again."

Customer Three wants:

1. _____

2. _____

3. _____

True or False?

___ Customer Three wants you to provide advice, when it is appropriate.

The answer is True. When there are choices between products, service, pricing, payment options, and other factors, customers may need your help. Be of even greater service by helping your customers make the right decision.

(Compare your answers regarding the three customers to the author's responses on the next page.)

CUSTOMER WANTS: AUTHOR'S RESPONSES

Customer One wants: (page 70)

1. dependable service

2. answers to questions

3. not to be transferred from one person to another

4. correct information

Customer Two wants: (page 71)

1. to talk with people who know what they are doing

2. consistent service

3. courteous service

4. a fast response

Customer Two said: when we decide to buy from a company we consider:

1. the product

2. the service

3. the price

Customer Three wants: (page 72)

1. to be listened to

2. to have suggestions offered

3. not to be put on hold

Interpreting Customer Needs

When you think about it, customers do ask for a lot. They expect a fast response, error-free information, quality products, courteous treatment, on-time shipments, and much more. If you were the customer, would your needs be any different from those mentioned at the bottom of page 70? Wouldn't you expect quality service? If the company you called failed to provide what you wanted, wouldn't you do what most customers do—namely, find another company to do business with?

CUSTOMER NEED	CUSTOMER MEANING
1. Listen to me.	Pay attention—understand me—hear what I have to say.
2. I want dependable service.	I need to know you will meet your commitments.
3. Give me correct information.	Don't guess at the right answer. If you don't know or have to check, okay, but don't give me the wrong information.
4. Do not transfer me from person to person.	Connect me with the right person the first time. Don't just get rid of me. Don't leave me on hold.
5. Know your job, help me, and, when appropriate, offer suggestions.	I depend on your knowledge. Please offer suggestions or counsel me.
6. I need consistent service.	Be dependable. Treat me like the important customer I am.
7. I expect courteous service.	Let me know you appreciate my business each time I call.
8. I expect action.	Don't make me wait unnecessarily. I know you can't always meet my demands but be as responsive as possible.

Attitude Is Your Key to Success

We have talked about telephone skills and what customers want, but perhaps the key to providing customer service is *attitude.**

Attitude is your mental position on facts—or, more simply, the way you view things.

There are five important factors about attitude:

1. Your attitude toward customers influences your behavior. You cannot always camouflage how you feel.

2. Attitude strongly influences your level of job satisfaction.

3. Your attitude affects everyone who comes in contact with you, either in person or on the telephone.

4. Your attitude is not only reflected by your tone of voice but also by the way you stand or sit, your facial expression, and in other non-verbal ways.

5. Your attitude is not fixed. The attitude you choose to display is up to you.

Making Choices

Whenever you talk on the telephone you have a choice. You can reflect a positive, upbeat attitude, or you can make another, less desirable choice.

It is not always easy to be positive. There are work situations that can have negative influences on your attitude. Someone you work with may depress your attitude, your workload may be heavy and produce stress, or certain customers can be demanding and even unpleasant to work with. All of these factors affect your attitude.

You have probably had days that you begin by feeling great. As the day progresses, however, your feeling of well-being starts to slip away. By day's end, you are glad it is over.

For an outstanding book on attitude, read <u>Attitude: Your Most Priceless Possession</u>, Crisp Publications Inc., 1995.

Attitude Is Your Key to Success (CONTINUED)

Taking Control

If you have had this experience, you are normal. However, even on down days, you have some control. Your control begins when you decide that *you* are responsible for the attitude you display. When you decide to be positive and customer-oriented, you have taken the first step. Your challenge is to maintain this positive attitude despite situations that take place throughout the day.

For example, suppose your first telephone contact of the day is with a very unpleasant customer. This provides you with a choice. You can allow this unpleasant situation to affect your attitude negatively for the rest of the day, or you can put the incident behind you and consciously regain a positive attitude. Every daily activity provides another "attitude opportunity."

It sounds easy, doesn't it? Well, as you know, it is not always that easy. However, you also probably know that the benefits of a positive customer-oriented attitude outweigh the alternatives. For one thing, with a positive attitude, your job satisfaction remains high and you will continue to provide good customer service.

Tips for a Positive Attitude

Here are some tips to help you establish and maintain a positive and customer-oriented attitude.

TIP 1. Start each day with thoughts about the positive aspects of your job.

TIP 2. When negative events occur, take a deep breath and re-establish a positive attitude by focusing on activities that allow you to regain your perspective.

TIP 3. Whenever possible, avoid people and situations that are predictably negative.

TIP 4. Share your attitude when things are going well. Attitudes are caught, not taught.

CASE STUDY

WHAT THE PERFORMANCE REVIEW REVEALED

James received a poor job performance review. His supervisor said his attitude toward customers was the biggest problem. This took James by surprise because he was unaware of the effect he was having on others.

James decided to try to improve his attitude. First, he made a list of what he considered to be negative impacts on his attitude. After reviewing the list, James realized that working with two or three unpleasant customers each day had a negative influence on his attitude toward other customers and his co-workers. James suddenly realized that although he talked with 30 customers a day, he was allowing a very small percentage of them to influence his behavior negatively.

James decided to improve his attitude by reflecting on customer successes he had already experienced following each unpleasant customer experience.

The next page contains a customer service attitude survey. This should provide you with feedback about your attitude toward customers.

CUSTOMER SERVICE ATTITUDE SURVEY

To check your customer service attitude, complete this survey. Answer each statement honestly.

(CIRCLE ONE)

1. **T or F** Customers expect too much from me.

2. **T or F** Customers should try to understand some of our problems.

3. **T or F** It is not reasonable for a customer to expect a fast response on every call.

4. **T or F** Customers are too dependent.

5. **T or F** Customers should not mind being placed on hold for a minute or so.

6. **T or F** If customers knew how many calls I handled every day, they would appreciate me more.

7. **T or F** Customers should show greater patience.

8. **T or F** Customers should understand why we can't help them when they first call.

9. **T or F** Customers are too quick to escalate problems to management.

10. **T or F** Most customers should try to solve their own problems before they call us.

Score 1 point for each false answer and 2 points for each true answer.

YOUR SCORE: _____

Answers are on the next page.

DEBRIEF: CUSTOMER SERVICE ATTITUDE SURVEY

All of the answers are *false*. If you scored a perfect 10, congratulations. If you scored higher than 13, your customer service attitude could use some improvement.

Let's review why the answers are false.

1. Customers do expect a lot of service. As a provider of customer service, it is not your job to define your customer's needs, but to respond to those needs.

2. Why should the customer need to understand your problems? They are concerned with their own problems.

3. The customer feels it is reasonable. Customers call when their work involves your company. They do not want to wait.

4. Some customers become very dependent on companies they do business with. This is exactly what you want. Customers who feel comfortable calling you will become repeat customers.

5. Try this: Look at the second hand on your watch, then close your eyes. Keep them closed until you think a minute has elapsed, then open them. More than likely you opened your eyes before the minute was up. A minute can be a long time.

6. The customer doesn't really care how busy you are. Customers want to feel important. When they call, they expect your full attention.

7. Yes, they probably should. Impatience, however, comes with the territory.

8. Customers want fast, courteous service. When they have to wait they are not getting what they want. When callbacks are unavoidable, arrange to call the customer at a *specific* time. Do everything possible to honor this commitment.

9. Some customers *are* too quick to talk to supervisors. When they ask to do so, they are saying, "You are not meeting my needs and I want to talk with someone else." There will be times when you cannot satisfy a customer. Discuss these situations with your supervisor to learn how they are to be handled.

10. Yes, some customers could avoid calling you if they tried to solve their own problems. But why should they? The customer's view is, "That's your job." Why spend time solving problems if there is a simpler way to get a solution? Be grateful when customers call.

— EXERCISE: RESPONDING TO SITUATIONS AND PEOPLE —

You come to work early so that you can spend some time on organizing. Your supervisor comes over and wants to discuss the "mess" on your desk. You explain, "That's why I came in early." Your supervisor says, "You should have taken care of this mess days ago." You explain that, "There have been so many customer calls I haven't had time." The supervisor responds with, "You need to learn how to juggle your workload better."

Well, what's your reaction to your supervisor? Check (✔) all that apply.

___ **I'm mad at her.**

___ **She's unfair.**

___ **I'm not appreciated around here.**

___ **She's ruined my morning.**

___ **My attitude is shot for today.**

All of these reactions are pretty normal, but to maintain a positive attitude we have to move beyond so-called "normal reactions." Maybe you're upset at the supervisor. That's pretty normal. But to remain upset for very long is not a good choice of attitude. So despite the unpleasant encounter with your supervisor, you need to choose a positive attitude. With a positive attitude the day will go much better. Just make the right choice.

Here is another common situation:

The first call comes in and it is an irate customer. This guy is so made it takes you several minutes before he is calm enough to tell you what the problem is. You have to make several calls to solve his problem and then you call him back. You provide a solution but he is still upset. When the conversation ends, he does not even say thank you or goodbye or anything, he just hangs up.

Well, you have another choice. You can be upset or frustrated or even angry, but then you have the rest of the day to think about it. If your attitude slips and becomes negative because of this angry customer, then you are in for a very long day. On the other hand, if you select a positive attitude the day will probably go pretty well. It is your choice!

The next unpleasant situation you find yourself in, take a moment and note how it affects your attitude. Then push yourself to choose a positive attitude.

Quality Customer Service Defined

Let's take a moment and define quality service. Be sure to keep customer needs in mind as you write out your definition. This is a good exercise for your work group to complete during a meeting.

QUALITY CUSTOMER SERVICE: _____

_____

_____

_____

_____

_____

_____

There are several acceptable definitions of quality customer service. However, one key phrase that should always be included in a definition is:

"Satisfying Customer Needs"

If you included this phrase (or one close to it), your answer is a good one. Following is the author's definition:

*"Quality Customer Service Satisfies Customer Needs
in a Consistent and Dependable Manner."*

It is important to keep in mind that we deal with customers' perceptions. The customer has a perception of the service you provide; you and your organization have one also—but it is the customer's perception that counts. Far too often organizations congratulate themselves on the service they provide without asking the customer. The customer is the only one who can answer the question: *"Are my service needs being satisfied?"*

We will discuss customer perceptions in the next part.

P A R T 4

Managing the Customer's Perception

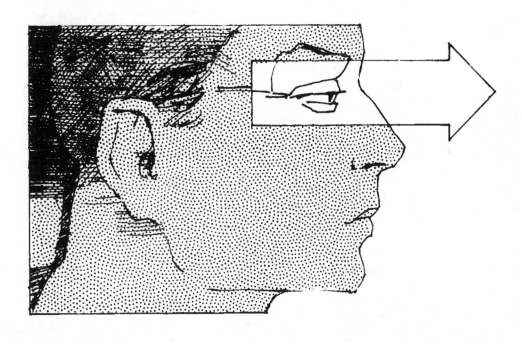

84

Create a Positive Image

The final section of this book is devoted to understanding and managing customer perceptions. These perceptions include how customers react to your attitude, your concern for their problems, and the way you manage their questions or service requirements.

When you provide service over the telephone, you may speak with the same customer many times. Even though you have never met this person face-to-face, you probably have an idea of what he or she is like. You may even have a mental image of what a particular customer looks like. Customers are no different. They also have an image of you.

Think of your favorite radio personalities. If you see them in person or on television, they often do not look as you imagined they would. The personalities of their voices have created mental images for you. Radio broadcasters are professional people. They create the image they want you to have. When you provide quality customer service, you are doing the same thing.

Let's quickly review the definition of quality customer service:

Quality Customer Service _____

Good customer service satisfies customer needs in a consistent and dependable manner.

CASE STUDY

THE WHOLESALE WIDGET COMPANY

You are customer service manager of the Wholesale Widget Company. You believe customer service is good because there have been very few customer complaints. The company is profitable and sales have been increasing. Despite this, you feel a survey of customers would be worthwhile to learn their feelings about WWC's service. A few weeks ago, you mailed several hundred customer service questionnaires.

The results were:

> 62% rated your customer service "average"
>
> 23% rated it "poor"
>
> 13% rated it "good"
>
> 2% rated it "excellent"

With these results, what attitude reflects your thinking as customer service manager?

1. 77% of our customers rated our service as average or better. *That's pretty good.*

2. Our average customer is satisfied. *Overall we need some improvement, but we are doing a pretty good job.*

3. 23% of our customers rated our service as poor. *There is a serious problem. We need to do something and do it now!*

This is a good exercise for your work group or it may be completed individually.

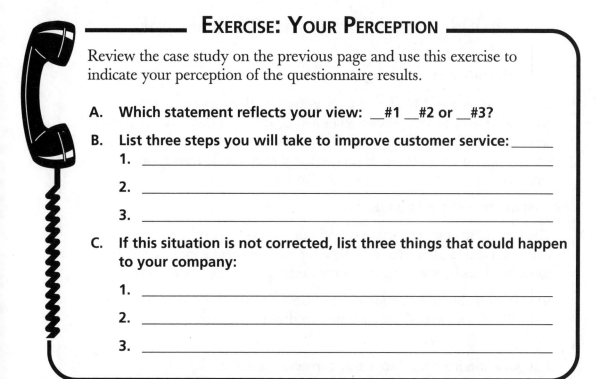

Exercise: Your Perception

Review the case study on the previous page and use this exercise to indicate your perception of the questionnaire results.

A. Which statement reflects your view: __#1 __#2 or __#3?

B. List three steps you will take to improve customer service: _____

1. _____

2. _____

3. _____

C. If this situation is not corrected, list three things that could happen to your company:

1. _____

2. _____

3. _____

YOUR PERCEPTION: AUTHOR'S RESPONSE

A. Which statement reflects your view?

The best answer is #3. *There is a serious problem.* Whenever customers are dissatisfied with service, something must be done. In this case, a very high percentage (23%) are dissatisfied. Before the survey you thought service was good. You were wrong. It is customers who decide how good the service is.

B. What steps should be taken?

The first thing you need to do is find out why your customers are not satisfied. Next, a plan should be developed to address specific customer concerns. Finally, it will be necessary to implement and monitor this plan.

Your answer should be similar to the above. As customer service manager, you will need a method for customer feedback to insure your plan is working.

C. If your service situation is not corrected, what could happen to the company?

When customers are not satisfied, they will take their business elsewhere. Sales will fall and profits will tumble. Customers will mention their poor experience to others and the reputation of the company will suffer. Ultimately there will be fewer jobs, smaller pay increases, and less opportunity for all.

EXERCISE: THE CUSTOMER'S PERCEPTION

Following is a list of telephone statements that have been made to customers. Read each statement and rate the *perception* you think a customer would have after hearing the statement.

G = Customer reaction would be GOOD
P = Customer reaction would be POOR

RATING

1. ____ "Good morning, Wholesale Widget Company, Jim Smith speaking. May I help you?"

2. ____ "Sorry, that's not my job. You will have to call tech support."

3. ____ "Good morning, Wholesale Widget."

4. ____ "Mark is out. Any message?"

5. ____ "Thanks for your order."

6. ____ "I don't work in that department, so I can't help you."

7. ____ "Good morning, customer service."

8. ____ "I really don't know why our service person didn't return your call. Did you try to call him back?"

9. ____ "I'm sorry it took so long to get back to you. I'm sure we can solve your problem with this call. Now, how may I help you?"

10. ____ "May I review your order to insure we have all of the information?"

11. ____ "Whom were you holding for?"

12. ____ "Thanks for calling."

13. ____ "Mr. Smith, I'm sorry you received the wrong material, but I wrote the order down just as you gave it to me."

THE CUSTOMER'S PERCEPTION: AUTHOR'S RESPONSE

1. "Good morning, Wholesale Widget Company, Jim Smith speaking. May I help you?"

   Perception rating: **GOOD.** The telephone was answered using the four courtesy points:

   - A greeting

   - Statement of company name

   - Your name

   - An offer of help

   If an incoming call has been answered previously by a receptionist, there is no need to restate the organization name. In this case the department or group name should be used.

2. "Sorry, that's not my job. You will have to call tech support."

   Perception rating: **POOR.** This statement will only frustrate the customer.

3. "Good morning, Wholesale Widget."

   Perception rating: **POOR.** If a receptionist made this statement, it would be acceptable if an offer to help were included. In telephone situations in which a call is answered at a central point and then routed to the requested individual or department, there is no need for a personal introduction. In all other cases, however, it is important to let the customer know to whom they are speaking.

4. "Mark is out. Any message?"

   Perception rating: **POOR.** If you change the phrase to "May I take a message?" it would be more acceptable.

5. "Thanks for your order."

   Perception rating: **GOOD.** This simple statement should always be used when the customer places an order.

6. "I don't work in that department, so I can't help you."

    Perception rating: **POOR.** Even though you do not work in that department and cannot help the customer, there is no excuse for not offering to help by transferring the call or taking a message.

7. "Good morning, customer service."

    Perception rating: **POOR.** Two of the four customer answering courtesy points were omitted:

    - Introducing yourself

    - Offering help

8. "I really don't know why our service person didn't return your call. Did you try to call him back?"

    Perception rating: **POOR.** To provide good service means taking responsibility. This does not mean you have to personally solve the customer's problem, but you need to assure the customer that corrective action will be taken.

9. "I'm sorry it took so long to get back to you. I'm sure we can solve your problem with this call. Now, how may I help you?"

    Perception rating: **GOOD.** An apology was made for slow service and the customer received assurance that the problem will be solved.

10. "May I review your order to insure we have all of the information?"

    Perception rating: **GOOD.** Accuracy is important. To repeat a customer's order or request is a good idea.

The Customer's Perception: Author's Response (CONTINUED)

11. **"Whom were you holding for?"**

    Perception rating: **POOR.** Not knowing whom the customer is holding for is a common problem. When this occurs, get on the line and say, "I'm sorry, I have forgotten whom you were holding for." Then write the person's name so you will remember. Whenever possible, provide the caller with a status report. For example: "Sally is still on another call. Would you like to continue to hold or may I take your number and have her call you?" Whenever possible give the customer a choice.

12. **"Thanks for calling."**

    Perception rating: **GOOD.** Always thank a customer for calling.

13. **"Mr. Smith, I'm sorry you received the wrong material, but I wrote the order down just as you gave it to me."**

    Perception rating: **POOR.** When a misunderstanding or mistake has occurred, it is not important to fix blame for the problem. The important is to take whatever corrective action is required to satisfy the customer.

Everything you say to a customer helps form the customer's perception of you and your organization. Your objective is to manage this perception so that it is always positive.

SAMPLE CUSTOMER SERVICE CALL

Morgan: *"Good morning, Customer Service. Morgan English speaking. How may I help you?"*

Customer: *"This is Wilson Erte from AP Systems. I need to order some new valves for our engineering department."*

Morgan: *"I'll be glad to handle that for you. What type do you need?"*

Customer: *"Well, the engineering department said they needed either the 516 or the 311 model. I'm not sure which one is the best. Is there a price difference?"*

Morgan: *"Yes, there is a 50-cent difference. The 516 is less expensive. How many valves do you need?"*

Customer: *"We need 85."*

Morgan: *"Do you mind holding while I work up a price quote?"*

Customer: *"No, go right ahead."*

Morgan: *"Your cost for the 516 would be $170.00, or $212.50 for the 311, plus shipping. Would you like me to explain the difference between the two models?"*

Customer: *"Yes, please do."*

Morgan: *"The 516 is our newer design. It is stronger and a little smaller than the 311. I think the last time your company ordered they purchased the 516. Would you like me to check on that?"*

Customer: *"Yes, would you please?"*

Morgan: *"Sure. Do you mind holding for a moment?"*

Customer: *"No."*

Sample Customer Service Call (CONTINUED)

Morgan: *"I'll be right back."*

Morgan: *"Thanks for holding. Your last order was in June and you ordered the 516."*

Customer: *"I had better double-check with engineering. I will have to call you right back."*

Morgan: *"If you like I'll hold while you call them. Will that be okay?"*

Customer: *"Sure, I'll be right back."*

Customer: *"I'm glad I checked. They want the 311."*

Morgan: *"So that will be 85 quantity of the 311 valves. Is the billing and shipping address the same as your last order?"*

Customer: *"Yes, it is."*

Morgan: *"Good, we will get the shipment out this afternoon and you can expect delivery on Friday. Will that be all right?"*

Customer: *"Yes, that's fine."*

Morgan: *"Is there anything else I can do for you?"*

Customer: *"No, that should do it."*

Morgan: *"Thanks for your order."*

Customer: *"You're welcome. Goodbye."*

Morgan: *"Goodbye."*

In this telephone contact Morgan provided the customer with excellent service. The customer appeared unsure about which valve to order. Morgan helped by explaining the differences, checking on a previous order, and then holding while her customer checked with engineering. Morgan was patient and offered every assistance she could.

Let's examine a few of Morgan's statements to see the customer perception they provided.

MORGAN'S STATEMENTS	CUSTOMER'S PERCEPTION
"Good morning, Customer Service. Morgan English speaking. How may I help you?"	She is friendly and wants to help me.
"Do you mind holding while I work up a price quote?"	She is courteous.
"I think the last time your company ordered, they purchased the 516. Would you like me to check that for you?"	She is offering her assistance.
"Do you mind holding for a few seconds?"	She asks permission before placing me on hold.
"If you want, I'll hold while you call them (engineering). Will that be all right?"	She is concerned—wants to help—provides courteous service.
"Is there anything else I can do for you?"	She offers additional help.
"Thanks for your order."	She appreciates my business.

EXERCISE: YOUR TURN

Suppose you were the customer. What do you think your perception of Morgan and her company would be? How would you rate the customer service she provided? Check (✔) each statement below that you think her customer, Wilson Erte, would agree with.

1. _____ I can depend on their service

2. _____ I received a fast response.

3. _____ I can trust their service.

4. _____ Morgan was very helpful.

5. _____ She listened to me.

6. _____ I was counseled.

7. _____ I received courteous service.

8. _____ The information was accurate.

9. _____ She understood my problem.

10. _____ I can rely on them.

Wilson probably would have checked all of the statements. In one simple telephone conversation, the needs of the customer were completely met.

PROVIDING ADDED SERVICE

In the example you just read, Morgan did an excellent job of providing service. But perhaps there was more she might have done if time permitted and if it were appropriate. Here are three examples of the added service Morgan could have offered.

At the close of the conversation the customer agrees with the shipping date and the order is firm. At this point there is often an opportunity to provide added service. Suppose Morgan said:

Morgan: *"Do you have our latest catalog? It has a June date on it."*

Customer: *"Let's see…no, I don't. Mine is dated January."*

Morgan: *"I'll send you a new one. Shall I send an extra one for engineering?"*

Customer: *"Yes, that's a good idea."*

Morgan: *"Is there anyone else who might need one?"*

Customer: *"No, I don't think so."*

Morgan: *"When you get your catalog, be sure to look at pages 32 and 33. Those pages provide a good description of the 311 and 516."*

Customer: *"Good, I'll take a look at that."*

Morgan: *"And starting on page 51 we have a new section on Andersen Values that I think you might be interested in."*

Customer: *"I didn't know you carried Andersen. We use a lot of Andersen."*

Morgan: *"We carry a full line."*

Providing Added Service (CONTINUED)

You can easily see where this conversation might be going. The level of service provided by Morgan is getting stronger as the conversation goes on.

What if the customer didn't have time and was not interested in the new catalogs? If you were in sales you might press on and try to get the customer interested. But as a service person you simply thank the customer for the order and move on to the next call. Let's look at another example.

Toward the end of the conversation, after the order is firm, Morgan asks the customer a simple question.

> **Morgan:** *"Mr. Erte, do you have other locations that might use our valves?"*
>
> **Mr. Erte:** *"In Pittsburgh, we have a pretty good-sized plant. They are probably using your valves. I know they use a lot of valves."*
>
> **Morgan:** *"Who would I contact at the Pittsburgh plant?"*
>
> **Mr. Erte:** *"Oh, let's see. I think Nancy Young would be a good place to start. Would you like her number?"*
>
> **Morgan:** *"Yes, please. I appreciate your help."*

Again, you can see where this call might be going. Morgan is about to provide added service for her customer's company by contacting their Pittsburgh location. Let's look at one final example.

> **Morgan:** *"Mr. Erte, I know you use a lot of our valves, but if you don't mind my asking, what other valves do you use?"*

Suppose the customer objected to this question and said, "I'm sorry, but I can't tell you that," Morgan would simply say something like, "I understand. Thanks for your order. We appreciate your business." End of conversation. Morgan is trying to be of added service. If the customer responds positively, she proceeds. If not, she closes the conversation. Suppose the customer responded in a positive manner. (They usually will.) The call might have gone like this:

> **Mr. Erte:** *"We use Davis, Milken, and also some Master valves."*
>
> **Morgan:** *"Did you know we are very competitive with Davis and Milken?"*
>
> **Mr. Erte:** *"You mean price-wise?"*
>
> **Morgan:** *Both in price and reliability. Our 612 Series was rated superior to both Milken and Davis. Perhaps I should have one of our salespeople give you a call and show you the reliability studies and our new pricing. Would you be interested in that?"*
>
> **Mr. Erte:** *"Sure, I'd at least take a look at them."*

Again, the conversation is headed in the right direction. In each of the examples, Morgan added service for her customers–added service that may also create new business. She accomplished this by simply asking a "lead-in" question at the right time during the customer conversation. You can do the same thing.

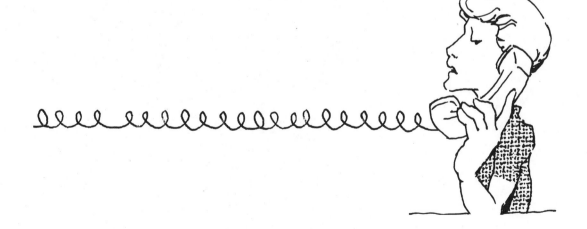

EXERCISE: LEAD-IN QUESTIONS

Make a list of lead-in questions that you can use. This may be a good exercise for your work group.

Morgan's lead-in questions were:

"Do you have our latest catalog?"

"Do you have other locations that might use our valves?"

"What other valves do you use?"

Your lead-in questions:

_____

_____

_____

TELEPHONE SERVICE SKILLS INVENTORY

The kind of service you provide is up to you. If your objective is to become a professional customer service provider, two things must be done. First you need to assess your present skill level to determine where improvement is needed. Next you need to develop a personal action plan to improve your skills. These steps can be done using this page, and the action plan that follows with the help of your supervisor.

Grade yourself on each skill area using the scale below. For a double-check, ask your supervisor to provide his or her opinion on your self-scored assessments.

5=Excellent   4=Good   3=Average   2=Below average   1=Poor

TELEPHONE SKILLS

___ **Handling the telephone**

___ **Mastering voice inflection**

___ **Addressing the caller (the different ways)**

___ **Answering the telephone (using the four answering courtesies)**

___ **Practicing effective listening**

___ **Managing objections**

___ **Learning the art of negotiation**

___ **Making the service follow-up call**

___ **Asking questions (using open and closed questions)**

___ **Making the outbound service call**

___ **Delivering bad news**

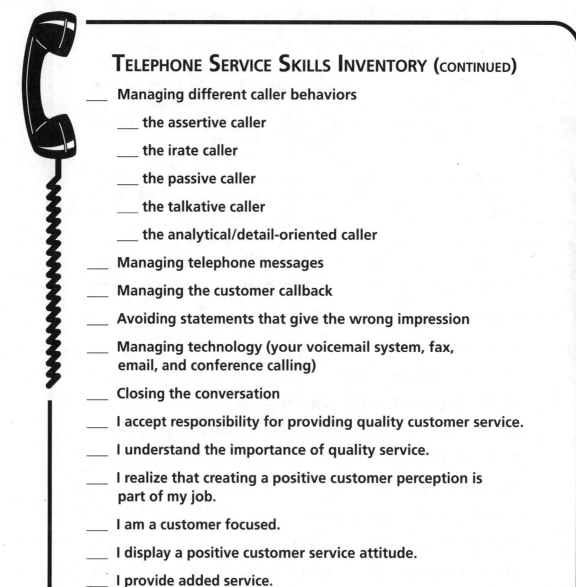

TELEPHONE SERVICE SKILLS INVENTORY (CONTINUED)

___ **Managing different caller behaviors**

   ___ **the assertive caller**

   ___ **the irate caller**

   ___ **the passive caller**

   ___ **the talkative caller**

   ___ **the analytical/detail-oriented caller**

___ **Managing telephone messages**

___ **Managing the customer callback**

___ **Avoiding statements that give the wrong impression**

___ **Managing technology (your voicemail system, fax, email, and conference calling)**

___ **Closing the conversation**

___ **I accept responsibility for providing quality customer service.**

___ **I understand the importance of quality service.**

___ **I realize that creating a positive customer perception is part of my job.**

___ **I am a customer focused.**

___ **I display a positive customer service attitude.**

___ **I provide added service.**

Develop a personal action plan for better customer service on the next page.

YOUR ACTION PLAN FOR BETTER CUSTOMER SERVICE

Your personal action plan will be developed in four steps:

STEP 1. List all skill areas you rated as 3, 2, or 1 on pages 101–102.

_____

_____

_____

_____

_____

_____

_____

_____

_____

_____

_____

STEP 2. Circle your *five* most critical skill areas above that need
        improvement.

Your Action Plan for Better Customer Service (CONTINUED)

STEP 3. Write down an action plan to improve the five skills. Include specific activities and dates you plan to start and complete. Activities might include reading more about the skill area, observing a more experienced co-worker, watching training videos, adding more concentration and effort when applying the skill, and discussing the skill area with your supervisor.

SKILL AREA	IMPROVEMENT ACTIVITY	START	COMPLETE
1. _____	_____	_____	_____
2. _____	_____	_____	_____
3. _____	_____	_____	_____
4. _____	_____	_____	_____
5. _____	_____	_____	_____

STEP 4: Review steps 1, 2, and 3 with your supervisor and commit to a date to review progress on your action plan.

Once you have made progress with the first five skill areas, you can develop an action plan for any remaining skill areas rated 3, 2, or 1. If you want to be the very best, keep working on your action plan until you rate yourself a solid 5 in every skill area. Step away from the crowd and make a commitment to yourself to become a professional. Good luck!

Now Available From

CRISP.
Learning™

Books • Videos • CD-ROMs • Computer-Based Training Products

Subject Areas Include:

Management
Human Resources
Communication Skills
Personal Development
Marketing/Sales
Organizational Development
Customer Service/Quality
Computer Skills
Small Business and Entrepreneurship
Adult Literacy and Learning
Life Planning and Retirement

CRISP WORLDWIDE DISTRIBUTION

English language books are distributed worldwide. Major international distributors include:

ASIA/PACIFIC

Australia/New Zealand: In Learning, PO Box 1051, Springwood QLD, Brisbane, Australia 4127   Tel: 61-7-3-841-2286, Facsimile: 61-7-3-841-1580
ATTN: Messrs. Richard/Robert Gordon

Malaysia, Philippines, Singapore: Epsys Pte Ltd., 540 Sims Ave #04-01, Sims Avenue Centre, 387603, Singapore   Tel: 65-747-1964, Facsimile: 65-747-0162 ATTN: Mr. Jack Chin

Hong Kong/Mainland China: Crisp Learning Solutions, 18/F Honest Motors Building 9-11 Leighton Rd., Causeway Bay, Hong Kong   Tel: 852-2915-7119, Facsimile: 852-2865-2815 ATTN: Ms. Grace Lee

Japan: Phoenix Associates, Believe Mita Bldg., 8th Floor 3-43-16 Shiba, Minato-ku, Tokyo 105-0014, Japan   Tel: 81-3-5427-6231, Facsimile: 81-3-5427-6232
ATTN: Mr. Peter Owans

CANADA

Crisp Learning Canada, 60 Briarwood Avenue, Mississauga, ON L5G 3N6 Canada
Tel: 905-274-5678, Facsimile: 905-278-2801
ATTN: Mr. Steve Connolly

EUROPEAN UNION

England: Flex Learning Media, Ltd., 9-15 Hitchin Street,
Baldock, Hertfordshire, SG7 6AL, England
Tel: 44-1-46-289-6000, Facsimile: 44-1-46-289-2417   ATTN: Mr. David Willetts

INDIA

Multi-Media HRD, Pvt. Ltd., National House, Floor 1
6 Tulloch Road, Appolo Bunder, Bombay, India 400-039
Tel: 91-22-204-2281, Facsimile: 91-22-283-6478
ATTN: Messrs. Ajay Aggarwal/ C.L. Aggarwal

SOUTH AMERICA

Mexico: Grupo Editorial Iberoamerica, Nebraska 199, Col. Napoles, 03810 Mexico, D.F.
Tel: 525-523-0994, Facsimile: 525-543-1173   ATTN: Señor Nicholas Grepe

SOUTH AFRICA

Bookstores: Alternative Books, PO Box 1345, Ferndale 2160, South Africa
Tel: 27-11-792-7730, Facsimile: 27-11-792-7787   ATTN: Mr. Vernon de Haas

Corporate: Learning Resources, P.O. Box 2806, Parklands, Johannesburg 2121, South Africa, Tel: 27-21-531-2923, Facsimile: 27-21-531-2944 ATTN: Mr. Ricky Robinson

MIDDLE EAST

Edutech Middle East, L.L.C., PO Box 52334, Dubai U.A.E.
Tel: 971-4-359-1222, Facsimile: 971-4-359-6500   ATTN: Mr. A.S.F. Karim